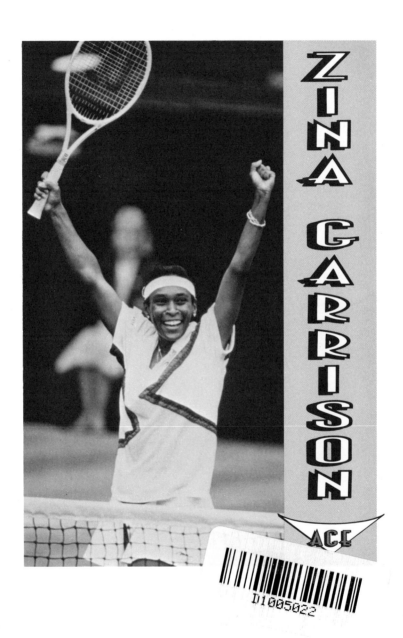

ZINA GARRISON

ACE

ZINA GARRISON

ACE

A. P. Porter

 Lerner Publications Company ■ Minneapolis

For the African Diaspora—A. P. P.

This book is available in two editions:
Library binding by Lerner Publications Company
Soft cover by First Avenue Editions
241 First Avenue North
Minneapolis, MN 55401

LIBRARY OF CONGRESS CATALOGING-IN-PUBLICATION DATA

Porter, A.P.
    Zina Garrison : ace / A. P. Porter.
        p.   cm.   —(The Achievers)
    Summary: Describes the life of the outstanding tennis player
who, in 1990, became the first African-American woman in
thirty-two years to reach the singles final at Wimbledon.
    ISBN 0-8225-0499-5
    1. Garrison, Zina, 1963-   —Juvenile literature. 2. Tennis
players—United   States—Biography—Juvenile   literature.
3. Women tennis players—United States—Biography—Juvenile
literature. [1. Garrison, Zina, 1963-   . 2. Tennis players. 3. Afro-
Americans—Biography.] I. Title. II. Series.
GV994.G37P67   1991
796.342'092—dc20
[B]   91-22475
[92]   CIP
                                                                    AC

Copyright ©1991 by Lerner Publications Company

All rights reserved. International copyright secured. No part of this book
may be reproduced or transmitted in any form or by any means, electronic
or mechanical, including photocopying and recording, or by any information
storage or retrieval system, without permission in writing from the publisher,
except for the inclusion of brief quotations in an acknowledged review.

Manufactured in the United States of America

International Standard Book Number: 0-8225-0499-5 (lib. bdg.)
International Standard Book Number: 0-8225-9596-6 (pbk.)
Library of Congress Catalog Card Number: 91-22475

1 2 3 4 5 6 7 8 9 10 00 99 98 97 96 95 94 93 92 91

Contents

Grand Slam

"I'm coming into my own." — Zina Garrison[1]

"I'm sweating already just thinking about it." — Martina Navratilova[2]

"Once you get to a final like this on grass, anything can happen." — Zina[3]

"I'll just try to not hyperventilate when I get out there." — Martina[4]

"I've beaten her once. . . ." — Zina[5]

". . . And she can do it again." — Martina[6]

[1]*Houston Chronicle*, July 6, 1990.
[2]*Houston Post*, July 7, 1990.
[3]*Houston Post*, July 7, 1990.
[4]*Houston Post*, July 7, 1990.
[5]*Houston Post*, July 7, 1990.
[6]*New York Times*, July 6, 1990.

As the women's singles competition at Wimbledon got under way, the odds against Zina Garrison were 80-1. The experts figured that if Zina did her best at Wimbledon 81 times, she'd win the championship once. She'd never even made it all the way to a final match before.

To get to the final, Zina had to beat Monica Seles, the hotshot from Yugoslavia who had won 36 matches in a row; and Steffi Graf, the number-one player in the world and the defending singles champion. Then Zina would face Martina Navratilova, who had won the Wimbledon championship eight times and wanted a ninth title so badly she could taste it.

In addition to the toughest competition in the world, Zina had a reputation as a "choker." She had been in a lot of tournaments but had rarely got past the semifinals. Her emotions beat her more often than her opponents did. Tennis observers expected her nerves to make the difference this time, too.

But Zina had a new coach and a new approach to tennis. Things would be different this time around, so different that no one would take her for granted on a tennis court again. No one would have a psychological advantage over her. This time, Zina had something new, something she'd never had much of before—confidence in herself.

This new Zina iced Monica's hot streak and made Steffi the ex–singles champ. Zina made it all the

Monica Seles, ready

way to the final match of a Grand Slam event, something she'd never done before and something no one expected her to do. She was the first African-American woman in a Grand Slam final since 1958. And she'd beaten two of the best players in women's tennis—Seles and Graf—to get there.

Centre Court at the All-England Lawn Tennis Championship at Wimbledon, England, was a long way from the MacGregor Park Tennis Center, where Zina had begun her journey. It was even further from her beginnings as her parents' unexpected seventh child.

Steffi Graf winds up.

Zina passes on her knowledge.

2

Tumorlina

Mary Garrison's body had betrayed her. The medical doctor had examined the swelling in her abdomen and said that she needed major surgery right away to save her life. A tumor, he said.

Unchecked, this tumor in her abdominal cavity would eventually crowd her vital organs and kill her for sure. Mary was frightened, but she didn't want to die of cancer. Mary agreed to surgery, and her operation was scheduled at a local hospital in her hometown of Houston, Texas.

Mary's mother, Julia Walls, thought differently. Maybe she didn't think much of medical doctors. Maybe she did. She knew that everyone makes mistakes, though. So she urged her daughter to get a second opinion, at least ask somebody else.

Ms. Walls had the right idea. There was a growth in Mary Garrison's abdominal cavity, all right, but it turned out to be a fetus. Forty-two-year-old Mary Garrison was pregnant.

That was in 1963, and Ulysses and Mary Garrison already had six children—four girls and two boys. The youngest was already 10 years old. The Garrisons were shocked, and the thought of another mouth to feed was daunting. But Ulysses was a postman, a good job for an African-American man in those days, and the family would make it somehow.

On November 16, 1963, Mary gave birth to a girl. To make it clear that she would be the absolute last Garrison child, Mary went all the way to the last letter of the alphabet and named her Zina. Zina's sisters called her "Tumorlina."

There hadn't been any babies in the Garrison household for years, and Zina was doted on—some would say spoiled—from the first.

Quiet little Zina's troubles began before her first birthday. When she was 11 months old, her father died of a stroke. Suddenly, he just wasn't there anymore. The family was devastated.

Mary clung to Zina and the infant's uncritical love. Dependent as only babies can be, Zina was nearly always with her mother. Zina said later, "I was always underfoot, tagging along. Not having a father, I felt like she was the only person I had."

14

Zina prepares for a practice session.

Zina's 21-year-old brother, William Garrison, had recently been recruited by the Milwaukee Braves professional baseball team. A few months after his father's death, while catching for a Braves minor league organization, William was hit in the eye by a baseball. His career was over. Worst of all, he developed a fatal tumor.

William died a lingering death two years later. The two oldest Garrison men were gone, and Mary had to go it alone.

Zina said, "My mother was so strong. She had come through all this death."

In the Sunnyside Gardens neighborhood where the Garrisons lived, most of the people were of African heritage, and nobody, African or not, had much money. Mary Garrison worked as an aide in a nursing home in order to support her family. When she retired after a few years, the Garrisons had to depend on Social Security payments for survival.

Her family's lean times meant nothing to Zina. After all, most people in the neighborhood were in similar shape. And as the much-coddled baby of the family, Zina generally got what she wanted. What *did* mean something was loneliness. Having no siblings near her age made her feel separate, different.

3

The Vision Girl

One of Zina's differences was clairvoyance—the ability to perceive things beyond the range of ordinary people. Zina knows things.

As a little girl, in the dead of night, Zina would sometimes leave Mary's bed and wander about the darkened house. Now and then she saw an image, a figure moving silently from room to room. Mary knew from her description that Zina had seen the ghost of her father, Ulysses, who had died so suddenly before Zina was a year old. In later years, Zina also accurately predicted the gender of each of her sisters' children. Her sisters called her the "vision girl."

Even as a small child Zina was a good athlete. Softball was her favorite sport at first, and she played it with the boys. She was so good—especially at hitting—that she didn't get picked last, either. Rodney Garrison,

Zina's older brother, says, "There weren't any girls as athletic as Zina. She always wanted to beat the boys."

"My sisters didn't like to sweat, but I loved to run and dance and play softball," Zina says.

Rodney recognized Zina's physical talent early and encouraged her to use it. One summer day when Zina was 10, Rodney took her to nearby MacGregor Park. Zina had sometimes watched the older children play on the tennis courts there.

John Wilkerson, a Houston parks employee, knew that the poor children around MacGregor would probably never get a chance even to learn to play tennis without a lot of help. The costs of equipment, court fees, coaching, and tennis club memberships make tennis an expensive sport. So in 1974, John had begun to teach tennis to local children for nothing.

That day in 1974, John saw Zina looking solemnly on. He says, "She was there for an hour. I walked over and said, 'What are you doing, breathing all the tennis players' air?' She smiled."

"I asked her if she'd like to come out and hit some balls." Zina could hit a softball just fine. John let her use an old wooden racket and found out she could hit a tennis ball, too. "Right away I could see that she could be a good tennis player. . . . She had hand-eye coordination that you don't normally see in a kid that age." And she loved it. She could run, jump, hit, and sweat all at once. Wilkerson had struck gold.

John Wilkerson coached Zina for 13 years.

In less than two—that's 2—months John had entered Zina in a local tournament. She reached the finals. She won the next one.

In her third contest, it dawned on John that not only did Zina love the game and the competition, she wasn't even keeping score. She read her opponent for clues as to who should serve. Zina was simply hitting the ball back. She was so fast and strong that she didn't need strategy. She didn't need a plan. She simply overwhelmed the other little girls she played against.

Lori McNeil was Zina's childhood friend.

Zina says, "I had never played tennis before. I just ran and ran, and tried to get the ball over the net any way I could. And I would never know the score. The match might be over, and I'd still be out there waiting to play."

"She showed great athletic ability early on," says Wilkerson. "Once she got that racket in her hand, all she wanted to do was play." And play she did, every day after school. All her brothers and sisters were much older than she, and they were interested in different things. Tennis gave Zina something to do, an outlet for her feelings and energies.

And her feelings and energies clearly needed an outlet. Temper tantrums were very much a part of Zina's arsenal. John says, "It was a problem for a while." He usually made unruly students run around MacGregor Park as punishment. But Zina loved to run.

"She's the youngest in her family, and I guess she was used to getting her way. And if she didn't, she'd let you have it. The turning point was one year when both Zina and Lori [McNeil] were 14, and we went to the Cotton Bowl Tournament in Dallas. They had to play each other in the semifinals. Zina just knew she was going to win because she had never lost to Lori before. But she got behind in the match, and then got angry and cracked her racket.

"I made her continue playing with that racket the rest of the match, and she lost. On the way home she was very upset. She asked me why she lost the match, and I told her it was because she lost her cool."

Zina learned a lesson and started to redirect her emotions. Her playing got a lot better.

At her first national tournament, though, Zina got blown away. She couldn't win one game. Some of the onlookers laughed at her. John even began to have doubts about his program. Then he said to himself, In life you have disappointments, sometimes humiliation, but you can't let that destroy what you've built.

Back in Houston, the pace picked up at MacGregor Park. Zina and the other juniors tried to play in as many tournaments as possible. The students and their parents sometimes sold chicken dinners to pay for travel costs. John often ended up paying hundreds of dollars per trip out of his pocket. He sometimes had to use his vacation days to accompany students to out-of-town tournaments, in addition to paying his own way.

By the time Zina got to Ross Sterling High School in Houston, she was maturing into quite a young lady. No more tantrums.

In 1978, Zina reached the finals of the Girls' 14 National Tournament in Birmingham, Alabama. She lost a controversial match in split sets to Andrea Jaeger. Even the almost entirely non-Black crowd frequently booed the line calls of the match officials.

24

John and Zina grab a bite at a tournament.

Scooping one up

Afterward, Zina wept in frustration. She had played well, though, and everybody there knew it. From then on, she was ranked among the top-five junior girls in the country. In Texas, Zina was number one, the first Black female so ranked.

Zina kept plugging away, refining her game, practicing four to six hours a day after classes. In 1979, she won the Cotton Bowl Tennis Tournament.

The American Tennis Association was formed in 1916 because the non-Black United States Tennis Association didn't admit African Americans. The MacGregor Park players always planned their yearly schedule around the ATA tournament in Atlanta. John Wilkerson had won it once. In 1979, when Zina was

15, she became the youngest player ever to win the ATA Junior Championship. She was on top of the world.

Zina and Lori McNeil had been friends ever since they met at MacGregor Park. Zina remembers, "We hit it off right away. . . . We hung out together and did typical girl stuff. We'd eat together and get in trouble together. She'd spend the night at my house, and I'd spend the night at her house."

They had often played singles against each other and doubles together. They would even travel together to courts in other parts of town so they could practice on a clay surface. Their dedication paid off. Lori and Zina won the doubles title at the National Hard Court Championships in San Jose, California, in 1979 and again in 1980. By then, Zina was ranked number six in the nation among 16-year-old girls.

In 1981, Zina did something truly extraordinary. She won the junior singles titles at Wimbledon and at the U.S. Open in the same year. The International Tennis Federation named her Junior of the Year. Zina Garrison became the number-one junior tennis player in the world. The mayor of Washington, D.C., designated January 2, 1982, "Zina Garrison Day."

Also in 1982, Zina graduated from Ross Sterling High School in Houston. Immediately after her graduation ceremony she flew to her first professional tournament, the French Open.

4

The Inevitable

All along, Zina's insecurities and volatile nature had been affecting her performances on the tennis court. Her talents were such that she could frequently play well in spite of her insecurities—but not always. Her inconsistency kept her from reaching the top of her profession. "I know I'm inconsistent, but the fact is that I'm good," she said.

Zina had even slept in the same bed with her mother until she was 16 years old, and her dependency on that relationship had always been a major factor in her life. Zina's mother had tried to support her youngest daughter in every way she could.

Mary Garrison took pride in Zina's accomplishments, but seemed never to take tennis seriously. Early on, Mary admonished Zina for spending so much time playing tennis, rather than finding "something constructive" to do. She once forced Zina to miss all of the Avon Futures circuit when her English grade wasn't as good as Mary thought it ought to be. Zina resisted Mary's discouragement, though, and eventually Mary came around to Zina's way of thinking, sometimes helping Zina pack for road trips.

"I'd come home and tell Mama that I'd won, and she'd just smile," Zina says. "She just wanted me to be happy. Sometimes she came and watched me play, but she never did know how to keep score."

For most of Zina's life, Mary had been sick with kidney problems and heart trouble. Around the time Zina began touring as a professional, Mary was found to be diabetic. Zina said, "She had to take insulin every morning, but . . . she loved her jelly beans."

Zina worried about her mother almost continuously. She'd call home whenever she was on the road to see how her mother was, to hear her voice. Zina was always afraid that her mother would fall seriously ill when she couldn't get home to be with her.

By 1983, Mary Garrison was a very sick woman. In mid-1983, while hospitalized, she went into a coma. When Zina flew to the East Coast for the U.S. Open, with John Wilkerson as her coach, her mother had been unconscious two and a half months.

"I woke up, went downstairs in the condo where we were staying, and told John that my mother had

Althea Gibson was Wimbledon champ in 1957 and 1958.

died. I felt it. He said, 'You don't know what you're talking about,'" Zina recalls. She said, "I know. I just know." John reassured her, and Zina went reluctantly back to bed.

The next morning, Zina called home. Her family said that their mother was all right. Actually, Mary Garrison *had* died the night before, the very hour that Zina dreamed it; she had been revived through cardiac resuscitation. Zina's sixth sense had been right, but Zina didn't know it. Her family had lied to her.

Zina lost her match that day and immediately flew back to Houston. Mary Garrison was in intensive care. Zina says, "She looked like a little baby." The doctors said that Mary couldn't possibly recognize anyone. They said that the tear that Zina saw roll down her mother's cheek when Zina got there didn't mean anything. It was just a reflex.

Zina and her family were stressed to the breaking point. "Everyone was keeping watch by the mother's bedside in eight-hour shifts," John Wilkerson said later. "Rodney showed up at the courts looking for Zina. I guess she didn't sit her whole shift or something. Well, she wasn't at the courts when Rodney got there, so he just waited. When she showed up, he was really mad and he hit her. And it wasn't a little slap. He socked her with his fist."

"It was all under the pressure of what we had been through," Rodney said.

Zina, John, and a tiny tennis player

"For two and a half months our mother was unconscious and on everything from a respirator to heart and kidney machines. The pressure got to all of us.... We were one big storm. . . . It's just family. I'm not a violent person. We grew up that way. To me, that's just bringing her back down to earth."

Two days later, Mary Garrison was dead. After the death of a loved one, a survivor sometimes simply can't admit that the person is really dead. They deny the death, typically for a matter of days or weeks. When it came to her mother's death, Zina's denial lasted for years. She just couldn't accept it.

"I just kept telling myself that my mother wasn't gone, that she was on a long trip somewhere," Zina said. "I know that sounds weird . . . but it actually happens and it happened to me. . . . For a long time after her death, I had problems. . . . There is a part of you that feels like no one else really cares."

5

Bulimia

Zina became even closer to John Wilkerson. At the same time, she became suspicious of everyone else. She was sad and moody, going from friendly to frosty in a few days. She didn't show any of the usual reactions to the death of someone close. She never seemed angry or guilty or sad, at least not until years later. Zina shut up all of her feelings inside.

"I held it in, while it built up to where I couldn't control it," she said.

Oddly, Zina began to play tennis better after her mother died, perhaps as a way to focus on something other than her grief. Always a long sleeper, Zina began sleeping even more, sometimes 12 or 13 hours a night. Sleeping so much was another way to retreat from the reality of her mother's death.

Zina kept playing hard, and in 1985 she rose in the rankings from ninth in the world to fifth. She beat Chris Evert-Lloyd for the Sunkist Women's Tennis Association Championship that year and knew she had what it took to be the best. Zina got to the quarterfinals at the Australian Open and the semifinals at Wimbledon. She turned 22 years old that year, and her cumulative prize money totaled $274,470.

Zina was doing very well for a 22-year-old, but only on the surface. Underneath, she was coming apart. Usually lonely and often down in the dumps, Zina became bulimic. She began going on food binges. She'd eat mass quantities, bags, boxes, cartons of stuff—ice cream, cereal, cookies. Zina wasn't picky. Then she'd force herself to vomit.

Zina said later, "I had an empty space in my life, and the only way to fill it was with food, and then I'd force myself to throw up. I was throwing up blood. I was destroying myself. Bulimia doesn't just destroy your insides; it starts messing with your mind because you're depressed all the time.

"My nails were soft, my skin was bad. I had no energy at all," she said. She had a lot of courage, though, enough to tell John Wilkerson about her bulimia, which must have taken plenty.

John helped Zina find a therapist, and the therapist helped Zina find herself. "The therapist said part of it was a way to try to fill the emptiness I felt," Zina says.

"And part of it was like finding a way to hurt myself." Zina began to realize that her mother was gone.

In recalling her life before therapy, Zina said, "After big matches, I just wanted to pick up the phone and call my mother. It wasn't until [1988] that I really accepted it. It was the key to gaining control, to understanding who Zina is.

"The therapist made me deal with everything in my life—the bulimia, my mother's death and the men in my life, my tennis game."

While Zina was struggling with her emotions and grief over her mother's death, her closest relationships, outside her family, were suffering along with her.

Lori McNeil and Zina had been buddies since the early MacGregor Park days. They had hung out together, played tennis together, grown up together. They first parted in 1982, when Zina turned professional and Lori entered Oklahoma State University to develop her skills playing college tennis. College tennis wasn't enough for Lori, though, and she turned pro in 1984.

With Lori now on the pro tour, she and Zina gladly renewed their doubles partnership. Lori began getting the hang of the pro tour and improving on her top-100 ranking. At the 1985 Eckerd Open, Zina and Lori became the first two Black people to play each other in the finals of a professional tennis tournament; Lori won.

Once Zina's championship doubles partner, Sherwood Stewart became her coach in 1990.

"The crowd didn't know what to do," Lori said later. "They were curious . . . but didn't know who to root for."

By 1987, both Lori and Zina were doing well. In May, Zina was ranked 7th in the world and Lori 12th. Only an hour before the entry deadline, Zina and Sherwood Stewart, a fellow Texan and one of the sharpest doubles players in the world, decided to play in the mixed doubles competition at the Australian Open; they won. At the U.S. Open, Lori beat both Zina and Chris Evert-Lloyd. Lori was on a roll.

Then in late 1987, Lori told Zina that their tennis partnership was at an end. Lori had signed with a new management company, and her new doubles partner was to be the wife of the company president. "That hurt me," Zina said. "[But] I thought about it and decided that might be best." Zina and Lori's friendship cooled.

John Wilkerson had been Zina's friend, coach, and mentor since she had learned to hold a tennis racket. Zina was a big part of John's life, too. He had given up a lot of money and time for Zina's sake. Faced with choosing between his longtime girlfriend and Zina's career, John had chosen Zina.

"He kept me under control, but at the same time he let me learn from my mistakes. He was like a father to me," Zina said. Parents and children eventually disagree; so did John and Zina.

Zina thought that John was spending an awful lot of time with Lori. Too much, in fact. On the other hand, when John *was* around, Zina resented his constant presence—taping her racket grip, making her trip plans, seeing to things, hovering over her. John couldn't win.

So Zina fired him. "I'm at a loss to explain it," John said. "Maybe after all that loss, she thought, I'm going to leave him before he leaves me."

Zina needed a coach just the same, and she hired Willis Thomas. Willis knew John well and had seen Zina play since she was 11. Willis would do fine.

6

Queen, King

The changes Zina had made in her life, the steps she had taken, began to pay off.

In 1988, Zina and Katrina Adams won the Bridgestone World Doubles Championship. At Wimbledon in 1988, Zina for the first time beat Gabriela Sabatini, one of the best players in the world. She again teamed up with Sherwood Stewart for the mixed doubles competition. Just as they had in Australia the year before, Zina and Sherwood won.

The next month at the U.S. Open, Zina had to face Martina Navratilova. Zina had played Martina 21 times before, and Martina had beaten her 21 times. This time, Zina won. Known for her lack of emotional display on the court, Zina broke with her tradition and jumped for joy. And the best was yet to come.

Pam Shriver and Zina won an Olympic gold medal in 1988.

Tennis hadn't been played at the Summer Olympics in 40 years. All that changed in 1988, and the top players from the professional tennis tour went to Seoul, South Korea, to bring tennis back to the Olympics. When it was all over, Zina had a bronze medal for singles competition and a gold medal for doubles, which she won with partner Pam Shriver.

About the doubles victory, Zina said, "Out of all the years I've played tennis, that was the first time people actually recognized me, or knew who I was. . . . You can play tennis for so long, and then you win a gold medal and all of a sudden everybody is recognizing you." She later recalled, "They [the Olympics] were the best time in my life."

Things were going fairly well for Zina. She was starting to settle down. Her break with John Wilkerson was looking like a good idea.

Zina says, "It was time for a change. I felt like I wasn't progressing under John's coaching. I'd been with him for a long time and I think we reached a point where neither one of us could help the other." She adds, "John and I don't see each other very much, but I don't think there are any hard feelings between us."

Zina and Lori were friendly again. Zina says that the change in doubles partners "[gave] us time to grow up."

About the split between Zina and Lori, Wilkerson said, "Maybe it was time for them to stand alone.

Lori McNeil and Zina in 1987

Both are very emotional players, and one's emotional state affected the other's attitude, too. It also grew tougher because they were playing each other more and more, in major events."

Over the years, Zina hadn't had much of a love life. As a teenager, Zina said, "It used to bother me that I didn't have as many friends as other girls, and that I couldn't go to as many parties." Some years later, in 1986, she said, "I don't have much time for a real relationship, [but] I'm not worried about it. With all the travel from city to city each week, you really don't have time to develop anything. My career is the most important thing in my life right now."

By late 1988, her tune had changed. "Every time I think I have a boyfriend, something happens. I think men are afraid of me," she said. "I'd really like to get married and have kids." Maybe she had another vision.

In December of 1988, a friend of the Garrison family introduced Zina to Willard L. Jackson, Jr. A young Houston entrepreneur whose company handles hazardous waste, Willard says, "I was very attracted to her, but I didn't think I had a chance at getting a date with her. I thought for sure she'd be taken."

Not only was Zina not taken, she was ready to *be* taken.

"It was love at first sight," Zina says.

"Before I met Willard, I . . . wouldn't open up to anyone," Zina says. "But Willard made me feel secure. I have hunches, feelings about people, and with Willard there was no wrong in sight."

People around Zina saw the difference. Pam Shriver, Zina's Olympic doubles partner, said, "She's in love.

Just seeing her on the court and off, you can tell she's happier."

Willard and Zina didn't hesitate. They knew all they needed to know. Within a month of meeting, they were engaged to be married. Just like that.

"Surprisingly, Willis, my coach, likes him," Zina said. "I thought that was good, because Willis is skeptical of everybody."

Being in love was so good to Zina that her tennis game improved. Among other victories in 1989, she won the Virginia Slims tournaments of California, Newport, and Chicago; three doubles championships with Katrina Adams; and the Wimbledon Mixed Doubles Championship with Sherwood Stewart.

One of the most memorable contests that Zina played in all year was her quarterfinal match with Chris Evert-Lloyd at the U.S. Open. Years before, when they were teenagers in Houston, Zina and Lori had waited in line to get Chris's autograph. Now the 1989 U.S. Open would be the last major professional tennis tournament for Chris; she said she was retiring, win or lose.

Zina had beaten Chris in 1985 at Amelia Island for the Women's Tennis Association Championship, so they both knew it could be done. But the crowd wanted Chris to go out on top, a winner. Zina said that she had "about five people" cheering for her out of the thousands present.

Chris Evert-Lloyd retired after losing to Zina in 1989.

Never mind the thousands. There were only two people playing tennis. Chris had won 157 tournaments, more than any other player in history. Maybe Zina thought that 158 would have been one too many. Zina won.

When it was over, though, Zina was the one who cried. "That was the hardest match of my life," she said afterward. "It was so emotional. To be the villain . . . It might not be the way I want people to remember me." She needn't have worried.

A couple of weeks after her victory over Chris in the U.S. Open, Zina and Willard were wed in Houston. It was a big—make that *huge*—wedding. Zina had 10 bridesmaids, including Lori McNeil, Katrina Adams, and actress Robin Givens. Willard and Zina honeymooned in West Germany and Tokyo, Japan, where Zina played for the U.S. Federation Cup team.

Over the years, Zina had gotten a reputation for choking in the crunch. She could get close to winning the big one, but she seemed unable to see the thing through to the finish.

Zina's good all right, but the Grand Slam singles events—Wimbledon, the U.S. Open, the French Open, and the Australian Open—had eluded her. She hadn't even made it to the final of a Grand Slam singles event. She'd played in many, and won the Australian Open doubles competition twice, but never managed to get past the semifinals by herself.

Katrina Adams, Robin Givens, and Zina

Just after the 1990 Australian Open, Zina changed coaches again, hiring doubles wizard Sherwood Stewart, her sometime partner, to improve her game. "I believe in Sherwood," she said.

Althea Gibson, Zina, and Arthur Ashe at Wimbledon in 1990

7

Ace

Zina did well in the first half of 1990. Zina and Martina Navratilova won the doubles competition in Washington, D.C. Zina beat Helena Sukova in Birmingham, England; Zina and Mary Joe Fernandez won the doubles competition in Filderstadt, Germany.

Then came Wimbledon. Zina had little trouble with her opponents in the first four rounds of elimination, beating Samantha Smith, Cecilia Dahlman, Andrea Leand, and Helena Sukova in straight sets.

Zina's physical gift, her sheer athletic ability, is unquestioned. Most experts, including Martina Navratilova, have acknowledged that Zina is the fastest woman on the professional tennis tour, period. Nobody can move like Zina.

But Monica Seles had won 36 matches in a row. The 16-year-old Yugoslavian hadn't lost a match in nearly four months. On the other hand, Zina had recently lost in the first round of the French Open and was beginning to think that her Grand Slam chance might still get away from her. At 26, Zina must have wondered if tennis's teenagers would leave her any openings she could take advantage of.

At Wimbledon 1990, Monica won the first set of their fifth-round match, and most observers expected Zina to collapse under the pressure. But she didn't.

Katrina Adams, Zina's friend and doubles partner

Of her former shaky nerves, Zina said later, "Psychologists used me as an example of emotionally getting upset under pressure. I just couldn't handle it. I think since then I've grown a lot."

Zina came back in the second set of the match, playing hard and smart; she won. In the last set, Zina never let up, trying to keep her taller opponent off balance. Monica rallied once, but only briefly—even though Zina slipped on the court and strained her upper thigh. Asked by the umpire whether she wanted an injury time-out, Zina refused.

Rubbing her leg and moving slowly, Zina prepared to fight back. Monica bounced on her toes, anticipating victory. Zina looked over at her family and friends, took a long, slow breath, and in the next few minutes blew Monica away. Zina's powerful forehand shots won 11 of the last 12 points.

Zina lost her footing yet again. It didn't matter, though. Zina won.

After her match with Monica Seles, Zina said, "I've been in situations to win it and I didn't win it. I just kept saying to myself that I was overdue. I was just going to keep hanging tough."

Zina Garrison now had to face tennis's number-one player—Steffi Graf.

Zina had played in 33 Grand Slam tournaments and had never played for the championship. To do it this time at Wimbledon, she would have to beat the defending champion, of all people. As if that weren't bad enough, Steffi had won 66 matches in a row. She had beaten Zina the last five times they'd played each other.

A couple of months before, in May 1990, Zina had said in a magazine interview, "When I get people down, especially top players, I don't pounce on them like I should."

This time, Zina pounced. She won the third set and the match convincingly with a serve that Steffi simply could not return—an ace. Afterward, Steffi said, "I always said that there were other girls who could beat me if I didn't have a good day. . . . Tactically, she played a great match." She did, too. No matter what Steffi did, Zina had the proper response. In the final set, Steffi even seemed disheartened.

Even losing to Martina Navratilova in the women's final couldn't dim Zina's outlook. Things really were different. Zina's coach, Sherwood Stewart, said of Zina after the match that she had been "playing mind games. She just needed someone to believe in her."

Zina's mind games were over. A new husband, a new coach, new management, a new self-image, and a new outlook combined to allow Zina to concentrate better than before.

Sports psychologist Mark Heffenen said, "You could tell at Wimbledon this year [1990] that Zina was more focused and confident in herself than ever.

Zina and children at a tennis clinic in Harlem, New York

Whenever she stepped up to serve, her eyes showed that she had a plan and, more importantly, had the courage to carry it out."

Zina's clinics and talks with children give her a lot of satisfaction. In August of 1990 she agreed to be the national spokesperson for the YWCA's tennis program.

Arthur Ashe was Wimbledon champion in 1975.

Through the Zina Garrison Foundation, which she founded in 1988, Zina pays for valuable work with and for wayward adolescents, antidrug groups, and other charitable causes.

Zina says, "I love kids and I want to show them that a positive attitude can really make dreams come true—it did for me." At over $600,000 in 1990, Zina's winnings allow a lot of dreams to come true.

A few years ago, a shoe manufacturer chose not to renew its small endorsement contract with Zina. The company's officials, according to John Wilkerson, "said Zina didn't project what they wanted. They said they were looking for a blonde, blue-eyed white girl." The company abandoned seventh-ranked Zina for a white player who was ranked number 46.

About this kind of institutional racism, Arthur Ashe said, "If you're Black, seeking endorsements, you need to win a Grand Slam event; and if you can't win that, you need to win some [Virginia] Slims titles. After that, you've got to have an engaging personality. You've got to be able to walk into a cocktail party and work the room like a political candidate. You've got to have the personal self-confidence to meet people on a one-to-one basis and make them feel they're your best friend in five minutes. If you can't do that, you'll have problems." Zina had problems.

A spokesperson for the Oliver Group, then representatives for Zina, said, "A Black player has to be everything a white player is and *more* to be accepted, which is saying a whole lot."

After her semifinal victory over Steffi Graf at Wimbledon in 1990, Zina signed endorsement contracts—with a clothing company and other businesses—that reportedly totaled more than $1 million. At last.

Zina spends as much time and money on her work with the homeless as she can. She's also trying to get other athletes to help her raise money for homeless shelters as a part of Sports Homeless USA.

In recent years, Zina has developed into an attacking player, something new for her. Attacking players seem to mature later than those with other playing styles, and Zina is still getting better.

Zina's racket is now strung at 58 pounds, giving her less power and more control than the 48 pounds of previous years. Zina provides her own power, and Sherwood provides the plan, sometimes on index cards. Zina sometimes changes the plan, but usually doesn't feel the need to.

Moses Venson, Zina's trainer, provides the menu—less fat, more complex carbohydrates. Before a match, Zina might have oatmeal; afterward, maybe pasta with garlic and butter. Much to her dismay, Zina has far fewer pizzas than she used to.

Moses has altered her exercise program, too, at Zina's insistence. Zina doesn't work nearly as hard as she used to, but she works a lot smarter. Now she's fresher for tournaments and sleeps only 9 hours a night, rather than the 13 or 14 that she used to need.

Sherwood Stewart has proved to be a big help to the Garrison team, fine-tuning Zina's game with little adjustments—"about ten thousand," Zina says.

"She's got the power to blow people off the court," Sherwood says. "I want her to be so strong and intimidating that the other girls want to get off the court as soon as possible. [I want her to] make the other players feel like they have to play great shots just to win points."

Zina wants to have children, but not soon. First, she says, "I have some unfinished business in my career, and a Grand Slam title is on the top of my list."

Zina and Kathy Whitmire, mayor of Houston, Texas, share a laugh during the celebration of Zina Garrison Day, August 2, 1990.

Zina & Willard

ACKNOWLEDGMENTS

Photographs are reproduced with the permission of: Copyright © Carol L. Newsom, pp. 1, 2, 9, 11, 12, 15, 16, 18, 21, 22, 25, 26, 28, 31, 34, 37, 38, 40, 43, 46, 48, 51, 53, 54, 56, 59, 60, 64; Houston Chronicle, p. 63; International Tennis Hall of Fame and Tennis Museum at The Newport Casino, Newport, Rhode Island, p. 32; IPMA, p. 44; ©Eddie Wolfl, p. 6.

Front cover photograph copyright © Carol L. Newsom.
Back cover photograph courtesy of IPMA.